Celebrate!

Chinese
New Year

Mike Hirst

WAYLAND

Other titles in this series:

CHRISTMAS   DIWALI   ID-UL-FITR

Cover photograph: A Chinese New Year dragon dance in Singapore.

Title page photograph: A boy holding a lucky red envelope of money, a traditional New Year gift.

> **All Wayland books encourage children to read and help them improve their literacy.**
>
> ✓ The contents page, page numbers, headings and index help locate specific pieces of information.
>
> ✓ The glossary reinforces alphabetic knowledge and extends vocabulary.
>
> ✓ The 'finding out more' section suggests other books dealing with the same subject.

Find Wayland on the Internet at http://www.wayland.co.uk

This book is based on the original title **Chinese New Year** in the *Festivals* series, published in 1996 by Wayland Publishers Ltd.

Editor: Philippa Smith
Designers: Tim Mayer and Malcolm Walker

First published in 1999 by Wayland Publishers Ltd
61 Western Road, Hove, East Sussex BN3 1JD

© Copyright 1999 Wayland Publishers Ltd

British Library Cataloguing in Publication Data
Hirst, Mike
  Chinese New Year. – (Celebrate!)
  1. Chinese New Year – Juvenile literature
  I. Title
  394.2'614'0951

ISBN 0 7502 2530 0

Printed and bound by Eurografica, Italy

Picture acknowledgements
Circa 8, 13 top (John Smith), 17, 22-3 top; Eye Ubiquitous 11, 16 (Julia Waterlow), 29 right (P. M. Field); Robert Harding 4 bottom right (Corrigan), 6 (Adam Woolfitt), 19 top, 26 (Adam Woolfitt), 27 top (Jeremy Nicholl); Impact 4 middle top (Jeremy Nicholl), 4 far right and 25 (Christophe Bluntzer), 4 middle bottom (Alain Evrard), 27 top (Jeremy Nicholl), 28 (Alain Evrard); Occidor (Gina Corrigan) 5 left, 23 bottom; Panos 12 (Wang Gang Feng), 20 (Trevor Page); Hong Kong Tourist Board 10, 7 bottom, 14, 21 top, 22 bottom; Impact *cover* (Alain Everard); Topham Picturepoint 4 far left, 5 bottom right, 24; Trip 7 top (Moscrop), 13 bottom (R. Vargas), 15 bottom (H. Rogers), 21 bottom (F. Good); Wayland Picture Library 29 (left); Zefa 5 top, 15 top.
Border and cover artwork by Tim Mayer; all other artwork by Linden Artists; calligraphy by Erica Burt.

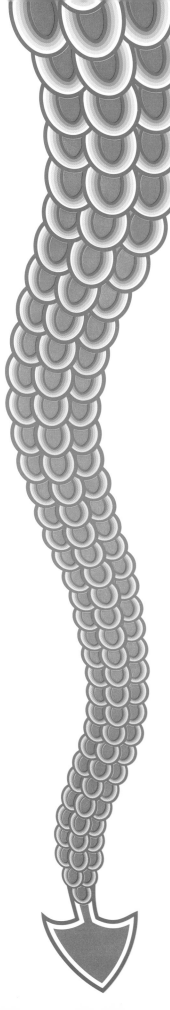

Contents

Chinese New Year Around the World   4

Happy New Year!   6

How the Festival Began   8

Religions and Ideas   10

Getting Ready for New Year   14

New Year Good Luck   16

Decorations   18

New Year Food   20

Music, Dance and Drama   24

The Chinese Calendar   28

Glossary   30

Finding Out More   31

Index   32

Words that appear in **bold** in the text
are explained in the glossary on page 30.

Chinese New Year Around the World

▲ A Chinese **dragon** in the town of Turfan, in China.

▲ People watching a lion dance in London.

▲ People bring gifts for the gods and light **incense** at a temple in Burma.

▲ A lantern display in Singapore.

▲ Farmers dress up as fat people with fat heads. Everyone hopes they will have enough to eat in the New Year.

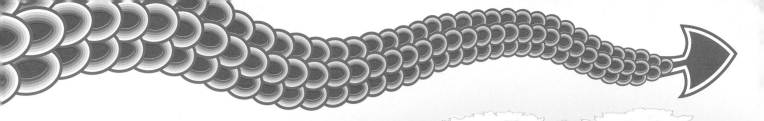

◄ A Chinese lion dances in the streets of Vancouver, Canada.

▲ A stilt-walking display in the far north of China.

◄ Preparing a Chinese dragon for a dragon dance in Washington DC, in the USA.

Today Chinese people live in many different countries. There are Chinese New Year celebrations all around the world.

Happy New Year!

Chinese people welcome each new year with a big festival.

Shops and factories are closed. People get together for parties and to give presents. Everybody enjoys the holiday.

▲ A New Year parade, with a Chinese dragon. The dragon chases a fire stick.

Firecrackers

Firecrackers are fireworks that make a loud 'bang'. Chinese people let off firecrackers at the New Year Festival. They believe the firecrackers will frighten away any ghosts and monsters, so that the New Year will be safe and happy.

◄ Firecrackers for sale at a market.

▼ Chinese New Year is a special time for children.

A lot of the Chinese New Year Festival takes place at home.

Being part of a family is very important for many Chinese people. They believe that each person in a family should look after the other family members.

Chinese New Year is also a time for friends and neighbours. In some cities, there are parades with colourful costumes and lion and dragon dances.

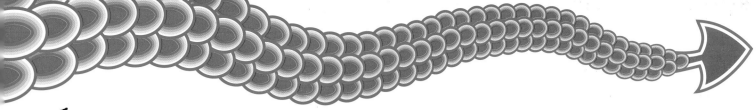

How the Festival Began

Chinese people held the first New Year Festival more than 3,000 years ago.

Farmers gave thanks for the harvest and prayed. They asked the gods for good crops in the coming year.

The New Year Festival is always in spring, but it starts on a different date every year. Today it is often called the Spring Festival.

In the past, the Chinese measured each month by the way the moon grows bigger and smaller. The first day of the Chinese New Year always has a new moon.

Chinese Almanac

An almanac is a book with lots of information inside. The Chinese almanac is called the 'Know Everything Book'.

Each new year has a new Chinese almanac. It has a list of lucky days in the coming year.

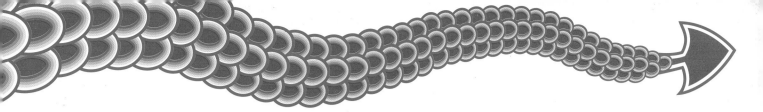

In China, every year has the name of an animal.

There are 12 animals, and each one comes round in turn, once every 12 years.

The 12 Animals

Chinese people say that your **personality** depends on the year you are born.

Rats are cheerful, but sometimes get bored.

Oxen work hard, and are patient and shy.

Tigers like adventures and are confident.

Rabbits like to be at home. Sometimes they are shy.

Dragons love to be free and are generous.

Snakes are sensitive and have a good sense of humour, though they can be greedy.

Horses work hard, and are **ambitious**.

Rams are gentle and kind, and take care of their families.

Monkeys are cheeky, but clever and successful.

Roosters make good friends, and work hard.

Dogs are loyal and caring, but they do not have a lot of patience.

Pigs are peace-loving and strong. They work well in a team.

Religions and Ideas

There are three great teachers in Chinese history: Confucius, Laozi and the **Buddha**. These men lived hundreds of years ago.

Today, many Chinese people still follow the ideas of the old teachers. The ideas help people to live a good life.

▲ People keep up many old traditions at the New Year Festival. There are special foods, cards and decorations.

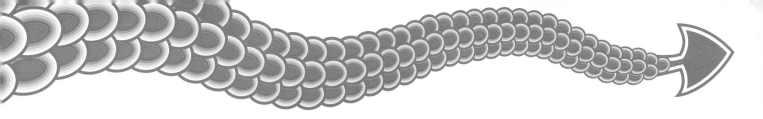

Confucius said that people should be brave, polite and honest. He also wanted them to learn as much as they could, so that they would be wise when they grew old.

Followers of Confucius always have respect for their parents and old people.

Laozi taught people to have respect for nature. He believed there are two forces in the world, called Yin and Yang. If Yin and Yang are balanced, people are happy.

◄ This temple has black and white marks on the wall. The marks stand for Yin and Yang.

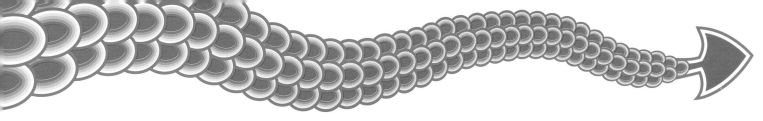

▶ A statue of the Buddha. Buddha lived in India, but his followers spread his teaching all the way to China.

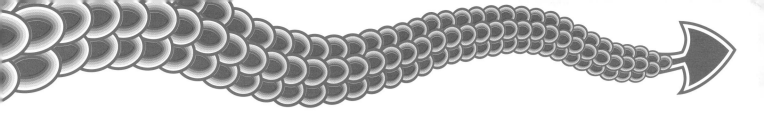

Door Gods

There are many legends from ancient China which tell stories about different gods.

These are the Door Gods. They were fierce warriors, who kept evil spirits away from the emperor.

Today, people still put pictures of the Door Gods at the entrance to their home.

Like Confucius and Laozi, the Buddha also taught people how to live a good life.

The Buddha said that people should have a simple life, and show kindness to all living things.

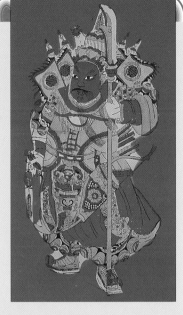

◄ A woman gives money to a Buddhist monk.

Getting Ready for New Year

Three weeks before the New Year Festival, families remember their **ancestors**.

They also eat a special meal of 'Eight Precious Rice'. The rice is mixed with at least eight other foods, including almonds, walnuts, melon seeds and dried apricots.

▲ Chinese people believe that oranges bring good luck at New Year.

One week before the festival is a time for spring cleaning. Some people paint their home, too, ready for the New Year.

Just before the festival, people also send cards to their friends. Sending a card is a way of making the friendship fresh and new.

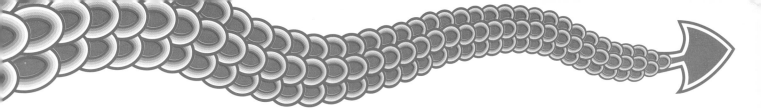

People buy new clothes in time for the New Year Festival. They believe it is important to start the year with new clothes.

◄ Market stalls selling red money envelopes, incense sticks and decorations.

Red Envelopes

Chinese families give presents of money to their children at New Year.

The money comes in a red envelope, with good luck characters on the front. Red is a lucky colour. It helps to make the children happy in the year ahead.

▲ The **Fu** signs on this card mean 'good luck'.

New Year Good Luck

There are lots of traditional ways to make the New Year a lucky one. Today, many people do not really believe the traditions, but they still have respect for the old customs.

► Knives and scissors are unlucky, so should not be used for the first five days of the New Year. If you need a haircut, you must have it just before the New Year Festival.

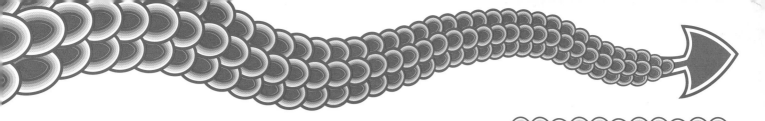

During the New Year Festival, everyone tries to be kind and friendly to everybody.

They do not use 'unlucky' words, like 'die' or 'accident'. They use 'lucky' words instead, like 'profit' and 'rich'.

Kitchen God

The Kitchen God watches over the family in the home.

One week before the new year, the Kitchen God goes to heaven to tell the **Jade Emperor** if the family has behaved well.

The family puts sweet, sticky food in front of a picture of the Kitchen God. They hope the food will make him give a 'sweet' report to the Jade Emperor.

◄ This calendar has pictures of the Kitchen God, his wife and children.

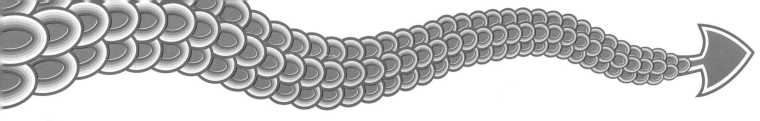

Decorations

For the New Year, Chinese people buy new pictures to put up in their homes.

New Year pictures often have oranges in them. This is because, in Chinese, the word 'oranges' sounds the same as the word for 'gold', and also for 'lucky'.

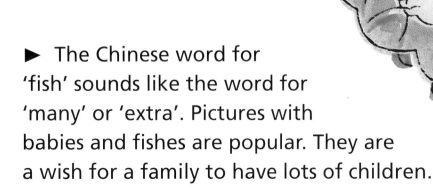

► The Chinese word for 'fish' sounds like the word for 'many' or 'extra'. Pictures with babies and fishes are popular. They are a wish for a family to have lots of children.

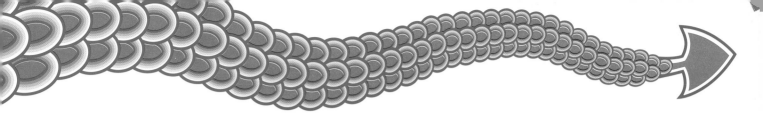

► These Chinese words make a poem. It wishes good luck to anyone who comes into the house.

Spring Couplets

Spring Couplets are good luck poems. They are written on red paper.

These are some couplets:

'May you have peace and safety wherever you go;
May you have peace and safety in all four seasons.'

'May all your wishes come true;
May your work be successful.'

Papercuts are another decoration. People cut delicate pictures out of coloured paper. Then they stick the pictures onto a window, so that the light shows through.

▲ Papercuts of animals.

New Year Food

Every Chinese festival has its own types of food. Some foods have a special meaning.

On New Year's Eve, every family tries to eat fish. At the end of the meal, they leave some over. By leaving some fish, Chinese people believe they bring good luck. Next year, there will be more than enough food to eat.

◄ Making dumplings for a New Year meal.

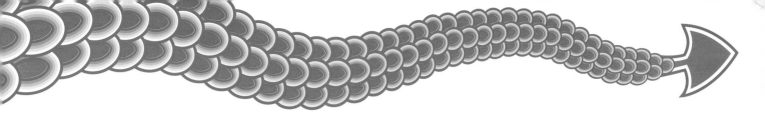

◄ Sticky cakes and dumplings for sale.

▼ Steamed buns are a favourite Chinese food.

The foods eaten at New Year are different in north and south China.

In the north of China, dumplings are a favourite New Year food. Everyone in the family helps to make the dumplings, which have many different fillings. Each filling has a different meaning. Peanuts bring long life. Sugar will bring a sweet life.

Sometimes people put money inside the dumplings, too.

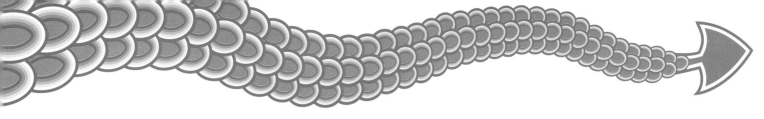

The main meal of the New Year Festival begins late in the afternoon on New Year's Eve.

The main meal is a feast. There are many different dishes.

On the next few days, people go out to visit friends and relatives. When they arrive, they always receive snack foods.

Favourite snacks are watermelon seeds, peanuts, fruits and sweet cakes with good luck signs on top.

▲ Bowls of sweets, ready for New Year visitors.

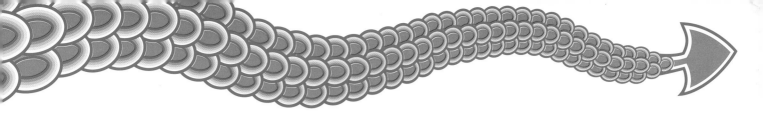

In the south of China, people eat more rice. At the New Year Festival, it is washed several times before it is cooked. Then it is called the 'rice for 10,000 years'.

Cooks also mix rice with sugar, to make a New Year's cake.

▲ A New Year feast, with rice, oranges, noodles and good luck buns.

▲ Men selling snacks at New Year. They are wearing red for good luck.

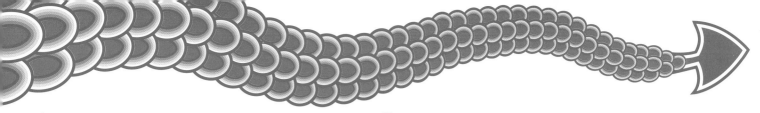

Music, Dance and Drama

Dragon dances are an important part of the New Year Festival.

In ancient times, Chinese people believed in dragons. They thought dragons were friendly and helpful.

Today, many towns have a beautiful dragon head with a long tail made out of cloth. It can take twenty or thirty people to carry the tail.

▲ A large dragon's head. People say that the dragon comes alive when its eyes are painted in.

Make a Dragon

Why not make your own Chinese dragon?

Find a large cardboard box. Paint it in bright colours, with big ears and eyes. Cut out a large mouth. The person carrying the dragon's head looks out through the mouth.

Find some old material to make the dragon's tail. Cut it into a long strip. Then, fasten the material onto the head. Two or three people hold up the tail as the dragon dances.

▲ Lots of people are needed to hold up this dragon's very long tail.

On the day of the dragon dance, the dragon dances all around the town.

The dragon follows a leader. The leader runs ahead with a large 'pearl' (a balloon or lantern) on a stick.

Some towns have two dragons. Then there is a competition to see which dragon dances longest.

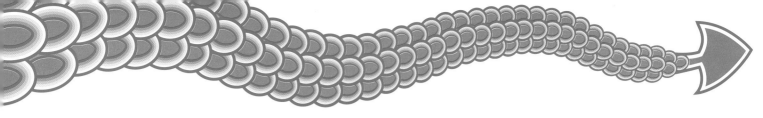

Some places have lion dances. The performers dress up in lion costumes, and dance around the streets.

Shopkeepers hang green leaves and packets of money outside their shops. When the lion comes past, it jumps up to grab the presents.

▲ Green leaves, oranges and red money packets hanging outside a shop in London.

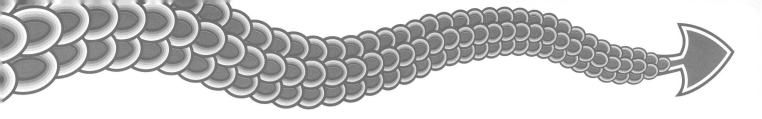

In the south of China, village people have competitions to see who plays the best drum and gong music.

As the music goes on, it gets louder and louder.

▲ This lion is taking a rest during the dance.

New Year Opera

The New Year Festival is also a time for Chinese **opera**. Each region of China has its own way of performing the opera stories. But the actors always wear traditional costumes and masks.

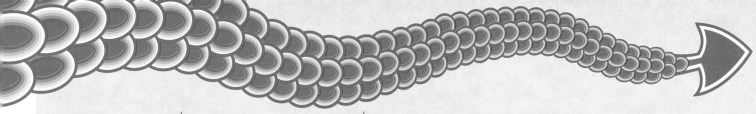

The Chinese Calendar

New Year is the most important festival for Chinese people.

New Year's Eve
Families get together and eat a big meal. They give red money envelopes to their children. At midnight, people set off firecrackers.

The New Year Festival carries on for fifteen more days. There are special things to do on some of the days.

Day 1: Chicken's Day This is a day for worshipping ancestors and gods, and for visiting relatives.

Day 2: Dog's Day A day for visiting more relatives and friends.

Day 3: Sheep's Day A day for visiting Buddhist temples.

Day 4: Pig's Day Married women visit their parents.

Day 5: Ox's Day On this day, people throw away any rubbish.

Day 6: Horse's Day Shops and offices open again.

Day 9: The Jade Emperor's Birthday People visit temples to make offerings to heaven, where the Jade Emperor lives.

Day 15: The Lantern Festival ▼ On this day, there are parades with lion dances and dragon dances. At night there is a display of lanterns.

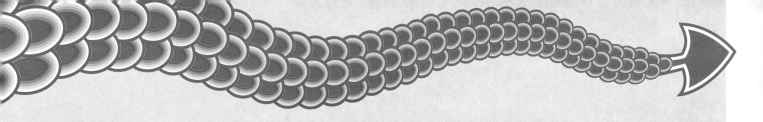

Qingming
(Pure Brightness Festival)

This is a day in April for remembering the family ancestors. People visit the graves of their dead relatives. They sweep the graves, and leave offerings for their ancestors.

Dragon Boat Festival ▲

This is always the fifth day of the fifth month. People remember the life of Qu Yuan, a famous poet who lived over two thousand years ago. There are dragon boat races on this day.

Mid-Autumn Festival

This is a harvest festival, and it is held on the fifteenth day of the eighth month. The moon is always full and bright on this day.

▲ Making mooncakes, round cakes with a sweet filling, for the Mid-Autumn Festival

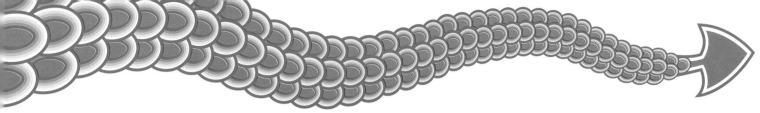

Glossary

ambitious   Someone who is ambitious wants to be very successful in life.

ancestors   The people who lived in your family before you were born, who are now dead.

Buddha   A famous teacher in ancient India. Some Chinese people are Buddhists, and follow the teachings of the Buddha.

dragon   A made-up animal. There are dragons in many Chinese stories, and they are usually friendly.

Fu   The Chinese sign for good luck.

incense   Scented substances which smell nice when burnt. Incense is often burnt at religious ceremonies.

Jade Emperor   In ancient China, the Jade Emperor was the most important god. He rules heaven.

opera   A play with singing. Chinese opera has traditional stories and costumes.

personality   The way you think and behave.

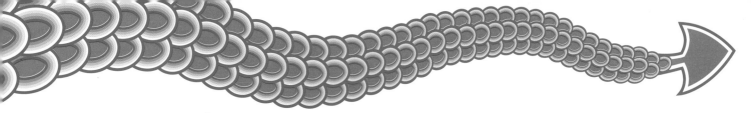

Finding Out More

OTHER RESOURCES

Chinese New Year (*World of Festivals* series) by Catherine Chambers (Evans, 1997)

Chinese New Year (*Festivals* series) by Sarah Moyse (Wayland, 1996)

Festival Worksheets by Albany Bilbe and Liz George (Wayland, 1998): 25 photocopiable copyright-free worksheets on the topic of festivals, together with teachers' notes and topic web.

A Flavour of China (*Food and Festivals* series) by Amy Shui and Stuart Thompson (Wayland, 1998)

Out of the Ark: Stories from the World's Religions by Anita Ganeri (MacDonald Young Books, 1997)

The World of Festivals by Philip Steele (Macdonald Young Books, 1996)

USEFUL ADDRESSES

Chinese Community Centre,
2nd Floor, 44 Gerard St, London W1V 2LP
Tel: 0171 439 3822
(Publishes books on Chinese culture in English.
Co-ordinates Chinese activities in central London.)

The Commonwealth Institute,
Kensington High Street, London, W8 6NR
Tel: 0207 603 4535
Web site address: www.commonwealth.org.uk/
(Organizes lectures, seminars and courses for teachers. Runs an annual course on the Chinese New Year Festival for primary schools.)

The Festival Shop,
56 Poplar Road, King's Heath,
Birmingham B14 7AG
Tel: 0121 444 0444; Fax 0121 441 5404
(Stocks educational material relating to festivals.)

Great Britain China Centre,
15 Belgrave Square, London, SW1X 8PS
Tel: 0207 235 6696
Web site address: www.gbcc.org.uk
(Publishes the magazine *China Review*.
Has a good reference library on China.)

Victoria and Albert Museum (V&A),
Exhibition Road, South Kensington,
London SW7 2RL
Tel:0207 938 8500
Web site address: www.vam.ac.uk
(Organizes courses on Chinese culture. Has a large exhibition of Chinese artefacts.)

Index

almanac   8
animals   9, 19, 28

Buddha   10, 12, 13
Buddhism   10, 12, 13, 28

calendar   17, 28–29
cards   10, 14
China   4, 5, 9, 12, 13, 21, 23, 27
clothes   15
Confucius   10, 11, 13

dances
  dragon dances   5, 7, 24–25, 28
  lion dances   4, 5, 7, 26, 27, 28
decorations   10, 15, 18–19
dragons   4, 5, 6, 9, 24–25

families   7, 11, 14, 15, 17, 22, 28, 29
festivals   6, 8, 28, 29
  Dragon Boat   29
  Lantern   28
  Mid-Autumn   29
  Qingming   29
  Spring   8
firecrackers   6, 7, 28
f   32 4, 17, 20–23, 29

        28

good luck   8, 14, 15, 16, 17, 18, 19,
  20, 22, 23

incense   4, 15
India   12

Jade Emperor   17, 28

Laozi   10, 11, 13

markets   7, 15
money   13, 15, 21, 26, 28

opera   27

papercuts   19
pictures   13, 17, 18
presents   4, 6, 15, 26

Qu Yuan   29

red envelopes   15, 26, 28
rice   14, 23

shops 6, 26, 28
Singapore   4

temples   4, 11, 28

Yin and Yang   11